# Rhythm
# Road

# Rhythm Road

## POEMS TO MOVE TO

### SELECTED BY
### LILLIAN MORRISON

LOTHROP, LEE & SHEPARD BOOKS · NEW YORK

**For my two Mimis**
**Mimi F.**
**and**
**Mimi H.**

3  4  5  6  7  8  9  10

Library of Congress Cataloging in Publication Data
Rhythm road: Poems to move to.
Includes index. Summary: A Collection of poems expressing movement in theme, words, and rhythm by a variety of English and American poets. 1. Motion—Juvenile poetry.  2. Children's poetry, American.  3. Children's poetry, English.  4. Rhythm—Juvenile poetry. [1. Motion—Poetry.  2. American poetry—Collections.  3. English poetry—Collections]  I. Morrison, Lillian.
PS595.M67R48  1988      811'.008      87-4071
ISBN 0-688-07098-1

## FROM MOTION

. . . the music
in poems
is different,
points to nothing,
traps no
realities, takes
no game, but
by the motion of
its motion
resembles
what, moving, is—

A. R. Ammons

# CONTENTS

# PREFACE

These poems are an invitation to what might be called a poetry workout. Reading them, we should be able to feel, in our pulse and in our muscles, the action described. Whether it is the twirl of a tarantella, the smooth glide of a Buick, the ticking of a watch, or the falling of a leaf, the poets have managed to suggest, and sometimes actually capture, the particular motion. They do this in many ways, not only by using accent, beat, and carefully placed pauses, and by controlling the speed, movement, and length of lines, but also by choosing and arranging their words and phrases so that the very sounds of the syllables resonate in us.

Often a poem will have much meaning beyond the motion, as does Judith Wright's "The Surfer" or Langston Hughes's "Dream Boogie." And in some poems, the sound is conveyed strongly and inseparably along with the motion, as in John Updike's "Player Piano" and Pieter Dominick's "Origami for Two." In any case, we use a sixth sense in reading the poems—what Roger Bannister, the great miler who first broke the four-minute barrier, calls "the sense of exercise." To get the most out of each poem, we should read it aloud, or at least hear the words and rhythms in our heads as we read silently. And feeling these rhythms and sounds, participating vicariously in the movement (which is sometimes subtle and complex), we add another level to our pleasure and excitement in poetry.

Because they have long been available in the older anthologies, I have not included a number of well-known examples of motion poems, such as Noyes's "The Highwayman," Browning's "How They Brought the Good News from Ghent to Aix," or Tennyson's "The Charge of the Light Brigade." I could not resist, however, the spirited "Casey Jones," or Poe's "The Bells," and Southey's "The Cataract of Lodore," which my father used to read aloud to us at home.

For reasons of space, I have presented only a few examples of the work of such poets as May Swenson and e. e. cummings, who have written numerous excellent poems of this kind. I have included anonymous folk material, familiar and unfamiliar, as well as the work of sixty-eight other poets, some from the past, but most of them contemporary, who successfully catch movement in their poems.

Lillian Morrison

# Rhythm
# Road

# The Twirl and the Swirl

**POEMS TO DANCE TO**

# TARANTELLA

Do you remember an Inn,
Miranda?
Do you remember an Inn?
And the tedding and the spreading
Of the straw for a bedding,
And the fleas that tease in the High Pyrenees,
And the wine that tasted of the tar?
And the cheers and the jeers of the young muleteers
(Under the vine of the dark verandah)?
Do you remember an Inn, Miranda,
Do you remember an Inn?
And the cheers and the jeers of the young muleteers
Who hadn't got a penny,
And who weren't paying any,
And the hammer at the doors and the din?
And the *hip! hop! hap!*
Of the clap
Of the hands to the twirl and the swirl
Of the girl gone chancing,
Glancing,
Dancing,
Backing and advancing,
Snapping of the clapper to the spin
Out and in—

And the *ting, tong, tang* of the guitar!
Do you remember an Inn,
Miranda?
Do you remember an Inn?

Never more;
Miranda,
Never more.
Only the high peaks hoar:
And Aragon a torrent at the door.
No sound
In the walls of the halls where falls
The tread
Of the feet of the dead to the ground,
No sound:
But the boom
Of the far waterfall like doom.

HILAIRE BELLOC

# BOOGIE CHANT AND DANCE

Ladies and gentlemen and children, too,
Here are four nice girls gonna boogie for you.
They're gonna turn all around,
They're gonna touch the ground,
They're gonna shake their shoulders
Till the sun goes down.
Hands up! Ha-ha. Ha-ha-ha!
Hands down! Ha-ha. Ha-ha-ha!
Got a penny, call Jack Benny. Ha-ha. Ha-ha-ha!
Got a nickle, buy a pickle. Ha-ha. Ha-ha-ha!
Got a dime, ain't it fine. Ha-ha. Ha-ha-ha!

TRADITIONAL

# THE LOBSTER QUADRILLE

"Will you walk a little faster?" said a whiting to a snail,
"There's a porpoise close behind us, and he's treading on my
   tail.
See how eagerly the lobsters and the turtles all advance!
They are waiting on the shingle—will you come and join the
   dance?
   Will you, won't you, will you, won't you, will you join the
      dance?
   Will you, won't you, will you, won't you, won't you join the
    dance?

"You can really have no notion how delightful it will be
When they take us up and throw us, with the lobsters, out to
   sea!"
But the snail replied, "Too far, too far!" and gave a look
   askance—
Said he thanked the whiting kindly, but he would not join the
   dance.
   Would not, could not, would not, could not, would not join
      the dance.
   Would not, could not, would not, could not, could not join
      the dance.

"What matters it how far we go?" his scaly friend replied,
"There is another shore, you know, upon the other side.
The farther off from England the nearer is to France;

Then turn not pale, beloved snail, but come and join the
  dance.
    Will you, won't you, will you, won't you, will you join the
      dance?
    Will you, won't you, will you, won't you, won't you join the
      dance?"

LEWIS CARROLL

# FROM WALTZ

Daisy and Lily,
Lazy and silly,
Walk by the shore of the wan grassy sea—
Talking once more 'neath a swan-bosomed tree.
Rose castles,
Tourelles,
Those bustles
Where swells
Each foam-bell of ermine,
They roam and determine
What fashions have been and what fashions will be—

EDITH SITWELL

# SONSITO

it is from the lips       from the lip blowing flying songy
it is from the maracas playing sheesheeshee to everything
to the base player who can hear whirling above his face

here they come bringing chocolate bringing heat
rubbing their shadows on the walking floor    out to the moony
light of secrets

'It is the wavy strength of ritmo'
you heard       you saw
son
son
sonsito

VICTOR HERNANDEZ CRUZ

# DANCE CALLS

Swing your honey like swinging on a gate,
Swing her round till she yells "Wait!"

Swing her fast, swing her slow,
Swing her round till she yells "Whoa!"
And promenade.

First couple out to the couple on the right,
The lady round the lady and the gent also,
The lady round the gent but the gent don't go.
Now circle four in the middle of the floor
And do-si-do like you did before.
Chase the rabbit, chase the coon,
Chase that gal around the room.

Allemande left with your left hand,
Right to your partners and a right and left grand.
Swing all eight when you come straight
And take her on home, boys, don't be late.

                                        TRADITIONAL

# DANCE POEM

come Nataki dance with me
bring your pablum dance with me
pull your plait and whorl around
come Nataki dance with me

won't you Tony dance with me
stop your crying dance with me
feel the rhythm of my arms
don't lets cry now dance with me

Tommy stop your tearing up
don't you hear the music
don't you feel the happy beat
don't bite Tony dance with me
Mommy needs a partner

here comes Karma she will dance
pirouette and bugaloo
short pink dress and dancing shoes
Karma wants to dance with me
don't you Karma don't you

all you children gather round
we will dance and we will whorl
we will dance to our own song
we must spin to our own world
we must spin a soft Black song
all you children gather round
we will dance together

NIKKI GIOVANNI

# THE RURAL DANCE ABOUT THE MAYPOLE

Come lasses and lads, take leave of your dads,
  And away to the Maypole hey;
For every he has got a she
  With a minstrel standing by:
    For Willy has gotten his Jill,
    And Johnny has got his Joan,
To jigg it, jigg it, jigg it, jigg it, jigg it up and down.

"Y'are out," says Dick, "Tis a lie," says Nick,
  "The fiddler played it false;"
"Tis true," says Hugh, and so says Sue,
  And so says nimble Alice.
    The fiddler then began
    To play the tune agen,
And every girl did trip it, trip it, trip it to the men.

Yet there they sat, until it was late
  And tired the fiddler quite,
With singing and playing, without any paying
  From morning until night.
    They told the fiddler then
    They'd pay him for his play,
And each a twopence, twopence, twopence, gave
  him and went away.

"Good night," says Tom, and so says John,
  "Good night," says Dick to Will,
"Good night," says Sis, "Good night," says Pris,
  "Good night," says Peg to Nell.
    Some ran, some went, some stayed
    Some dallied by the way,
And bound themselves by kisses twelve to meet next
  holiday.

UNKNOWN

# ATTIC DANCE

To the music of the guzla
light-foot Grecian ladies amble
through the maze of the romaika
for the pleasure of their lords.
And they find they're growing fonder
of the rhythm of the guzla
and the moves of the romaika,
all those leisure-loving lords.
And the guzla thrumming louder,
the romaika steps go faster
as the bare feet of the ladies
flash below their skirts of gauze.
As they raise brown arms, their bangles
make a sweet and tuneful clangor
and their lords rise up and join them
on the green and trampled sward.
On they whirl in fierce abandon,
clasp hot hands and dance in tandem
to the music of the guzla,
through the maze of the romaika
on the flower-scented sward,
every lady with her lord.

JOAN DREW RITCHINGS

guzla—a bowed instrument used in northern Greece
romaika—a modern Greek dance

Jimmie's got a goil
        goil
          goil,
             Jimmie
's got a goil and
she coitnly can shimmie

when you see her shake
          shake
            shake,
               when
you see her shake a
shimmie how you wish that you was Jimmie.

Oh for such a gurl
        gurl
          gurl,
            oh
for such a gurl to
be a fellow's twistandtwirl

talk about your Sal-
        Sal-
          Sal-,
            talk
about your Salo
-mes but gimme Jimmie's gal.

E.  E.  CUMMINGS

15

# DREAM BOOGIE

Good-morning, daddy!
Ain't you heard
The boogie-woogie rumble
Of a dream deferred?

Listen closely:
You'll hear their feet
Beating out and beating out a—

    *You think*
    *It's a happy beat?*

Listen to it closely:
Ain't you heard
something underneath
like a—

    *What did I say?*

Sure,
I'm happy!
Take it away!

    *Hey, pop!*
    *Re-bop!*
    *Mop!*

    *Y-e-a-h!*

LANGSTON HUGHES

# MARTHA GRAHAM

Earth and water air
and fire her body

beats the ground it
flows it floats it

seems to burn she
burns herself away

until there is no
body there at all

but only the pure
elements moving as

music moves moving
from her into us.

JAMES LAUGHLIN

# ARTHUR MITCHELL

Slim dragonfly
too rapid for the eye
    to cage—
contagious gem of virtuosity—
make visible, mentality.
Your jewels of mobility

    reveal
        and veil
            a peacock-tail.

MARIANNE MOORE

# Back Through Clouds

---

## POEMS TO RIDE TO

# FIRST SOLO

Giddy, I swayed in a Cessna
rising, no limit to the lift
the light wings found bouncing
through thermals. Sunlight
spun from the blades in a blur
I could see through. Lurching
along in the yonder, I looped
the hollow clouds, the wild blue.

WALTER MCDONALD

# JET

1-2-30-48 passengers to far vistas, lost in a trail of vapor

carrying

the winds

splitting

the sky

sweeping

turning

readying

steadying

plane

the jet

silvers

Up

JOHN TRAVERS MOORE

# OVER THE FIELD

They have a certain beauty, those wheeled
        fish when, steel
        fins stiff out
        from their sides
        they grope

over the field, then through cloud, slice
        silver snouts,
        and climb,

trailing glamourous veils like slime.
Their long abdomens cannot curve, but
        arrogantly cut
        blue,
        power enflaming
        their gills.

        They claim
that sea where no fish swam, until they flew
        to minnow it
        with their metal.

Inflexible bellies carry, like roe,
        Jonahs sitting row
        on row.
        I sit by the fin
        in

one of those whale-big fish, while
several silver minnows, lined up, wheel
        the runway
        way
        below.

MAY SWENSON

# THE ENGINGINES

The engingines
of the ailingplane
are st-tuttering
I hope they won't
beginnnn
to stammer:
30,000 feet
is too high for speech defects.

PAUL GOODMAN

# THE CALIFORNIA ZEPHYR

*(Lines on the Discontinuance of a Crack Passenger Train)*

The Burlington will now no more,
For the prairie and high plains run,
Take the knitted cars in clicking pride
*(Silver Tower* and *Silver Star)*
Out of Chicago sliding.

A blackbird in a cornfield sings:
*In silver no more sliding.*

No more now will the Rio Grande
At Denver from the Burlington
Take them for the mirrored day
*(Silver River* and *Silver Cloud)*
By the Colorado gliding.

A magpie on a green wire sings:
*No more in silver gliding.*

The Western Pacific will no more
   now
At Salt Lake City take
From the Rio Grande the last relay
*(Silver Castle* and *Silver Plume)*
Down the Feather River riding.

A blue jay on a boulder sings:
*Never in silver riding.*

ERNEST KROLL

# CASEY JONES

Come all you rounders if you want to hear
The story of a brave engineer;
Casey Jones was the hogger's name,
On a big eight-wheeler, boys, he won his fame.
Caller called Casey at half-past four,
He kissed his wife at the station door,
Mounted to the cabin with orders in his hand,
And took his farewell trip to the promised land.

    Casey Jones, he mounted to the cabin,
    Casey Jones, with his orders in his hand!
    Casey Jones, he mounted to the cabin,
    Took his farewell trip into the promised land.

Put in your water and shovel in your coal,
Put your head out the window, watch the drivers roll,
I'll run her till she leaves the rail,
'Cause we're eight hours late with the Western Mail!
He looked at his watch and his watch was slow,
Looked at the water and the water was low,
Turned to his fireboy and said,
"We'll get to 'Frisco, but we'll all be dead!"

                                         *(Refrain)*

Casey pulled up Reno Hill,
Tooted for the crossing with an awful shrill,
Snakes all knew by the engine's moans
That the hogger at the throttle was Casey Jones.
He pulled up short two miles from the place,
Number Four stared him right in the face,
Turned to his fireboy, said, "You'd better jump,
'Cause there's two locomotives that's going to bump!"

(*Refrain*)

Casey said, just before he died,
"There's two more roads I'd like to ride."
Fireboy said, "What can they be?"
"The Rio Grande and the Old S.P."
Mrs. Jones sat on her bed a-sighing,
Got a pink that Casey was dying,
Said, "Go to bed, children; hush your crying,
'Cause you'll get another papa on the Salt Lake Line."

Casey Jones! Got another papa!
Casey Jones on the Salt Lake Line!
Casey Jones! Got another papa!
Got another papa on the Salt Lake Line!

TRADITIONAL

# NIGHT JOURNEY

Now as the train bears west,
Its rhythm rocks the earth,
And from my Pullman berth
I stare into the night
While others take their rest.
Bridges of iron lace,
A suddenness of trees,
A lap of mountain mist
All cross my line of sight,
Then a bleak wasted place,
And a lake below my knees.
Full on my neck I feel
The straining at a curve;
My muscles move with steel,
I wake in every nerve.
I watch a beacon swing
From dark to blazing bright;
We thunder through ravines
And gullies washed with light.
Beyond the mountain pass
Mist deepens on the pane;
We rush into a rain
That rattles double glass.
Wheels shake the roadbed stone,
The pistons jerk and shove,
I stay up half the night
To see the land I love.

THEODORE ROETHKE

# TRAIN TUNE

Back through clouds
Back through clearing
Back through distance
Back through silence

Back through groves
Back through garlands
Back by rivers
Back below mountains

Back through lightning
Back through cities
Back through stars
Back through hours

Back through plains
Back through flowers
Back through birds
Back through rain

Back through smoke
Back through noon
Back along love
Back through midnight

LOUISE BOGAN

# THE CAR

Car coughing moves with
a jerked energy forward.

ROBERT CREELEY


# THE CARS IN CARACAS

The cars in Caracas
create a ruckukus,
a four-wheeled fracacas,
taxaxis and truckes.

Cacaphono-comic,
the tracaffic is farcic;
its weave leads the stomach
to turn Caracarsick.

JOHN UPDIKE

# BUICK

As a sloop with a sweep of immaculate wing on her delicate spine
And a keel as steel as a root that holds in the sea as she leans,
Leaning and laughing, my warm-hearted beauty, you ride, you ride,
You tack on the curves with parabola speed and a kiss of goodbye,
Like a thoroughbred sloop, my new high-spirited spirit, my kiss.

As my foot suggests that you leap in the air with your hips of a girl,
My finger that praises your wheel and announces your voices of song,
Flouncing your skirts, you blueness of joy, you flirt of politeness,
You leap, you intelligence, essence of wheelness with silvery nose,
And your platinum clocks of excitement stir like the hairs of a fern.

But how alien you are from the booming belts of your birth and the smoke
Where you turned on the stinging lathes of Detroit and Lansing at night
And shrieked at the torch in your secret parts and the amorous tests,
But now with your eyes that enter the future of roads you forget;
You are all instinct with your phosphorous glow and your streaking hair.

And now when we stop it is not as the bird from the shell that I leave
Or the leathery pilot who steps from his bird with a sneer of delight,
And not as the ignorant beast do you squat and watch me depart,
But with exquisite breathing you smile, with satisfaction of love,
And I touch you again as you tick in the silence and settle in sleep.

KARL SHAPIRO

# DRIVING

Smooth it feels
  wheels
  in the groove of the gray
   roadway
   speedway
   freeway

long along the in and out
of gray car
  red car
  blue car

catching up and overtaking into
   one lane
   two lane
   three lane

    it feels

over and over and ever and along

   MYRA COHN LIVINGSTON

# BRONCO BUSTING, EVENT #1

The stall so tight he can't raise heels or knees
when the cowboy, coccyx to bareback, touches down

tender as a deerfly, forks him, gripping the rope-
handle over the withers, testing the cinch,

as if hired to lift a cumbersome piece of brown
luggage, while assistants perched on the rails arrange

the kicker, a foam-rubber band around the narrowest,
most ticklish part of the loins, leaning full weight

on neck and rump to keep him throttled, this horse,
"Firecracker," jacked out of the box through the sprung

gate, in the same second raked both sides of the belly
by ratchets on booted heels, bursts into five-way

motion: bucks, pitches, swivels, humps, and twists,
an all-over-body-sneeze that must repeat

until the flapping bony lump attached to his spine is gone.
A horn squawks. From the dust gets up a buster named Tucson.

MAY SWENSON

33

# ELDORADO

Gaily bedight,
A gallant knight,
In sunshine and in shadow,
Had journeyed long,
Singing a song,
In search of Eldorado.

But he grew old—
This knight so bold—
And o'er his heart a shadow
Fell as he found
No spot of ground
That looked like Eldorado.

And as his strength
Failed him at length,
He met a pilgrim shadow—
"Shadow," said he,
"Where can it be—
This land of Eldorado?"

"Over the Mountains
Of the Moon,
Down the Valley of the Shadow,
Ride, boldly ride,"
The shade replied,—
"If you seek for Eldorado!"

EDGAR ALLAN POE

```
gid                     dy
up              gid
dy                     up
gid             dy   up
gid        dy   up
gid   dy     up
giddy     up
giddy  up    giddy up
giddyup    giddyup
giddyupgiddyupgiddyup
giddyupgiddyupgiddyup
```

JAMES MINOR

35

# WILL YOU COME?

Will you come?
Will you come?
Will you ride
So late
At my side?
O, will you come?

Will you come?
Will you come
If the night
Has a moon,
Full and bright?
O, will you come?

Would you come?
Would you come
If the noon
Gave light,
Not the moon?
Beautiful, would you come?

Would you have come?
Would you have come
Without scorning,
Had it been
Still morning?
Beloved, would you have come?

If you come
Haste and come.
Owls have cried;
It grows dark
To ride.
Beloved, beautiful, come!

EDWARD THOMAS

# WINDY NIGHTS

Whenever the moon and stars are set,
   Whenever the wind is high,
All night long in the dark and wet,
   A man goes riding by.
Late in the night when the fires are out,
Why does he gallop and gallop about?

Whenever the trees are crying aloud,
   And ships are tossed at sea,
By, on the highway, low and loud,
   By at the gallop goes he.
By at the gallop he goes, and then
By he comes back at the gallop again.

ROBERT LOUIS STEVENSON

# Wet Wet Wet

## WATCHING WATER

# OLD DEEP SING-SONG

in the old deep sing-song of the sea
in the old going-on of that sing-song
in that old mama-mama-mama going-on
of that nightlong daylong sleepsong
we look on   we listen
we lay by and hear
too many big bells   too many long gongs
too many weepers over a lost gone gold
too many laughs over light green gold
woven and changing in the wash and the heave
moving on the bottoms   winding in the waters
sending themselves with arms and voices
up in the old mama-mama-mama music
up into the whirl of spokes of light

CARL SANDBURG

# RAIN DROPS . . .

rain
drops
spot
they
spit
on
rock
they
rip
on
trees
rain
drops
tip
rose
buds
all
buds
wet
and
good
they
drip
on
hats
and

rap
on
cars
from
clouds
they
flute
down
with
a
long
sigh
and
a
small
song
they
kiss
your
hair
again
again
again
again.

SALLIE BURROW WOOD

# INVERSNAID

This darksome burn, horseback brown,
His rollrock highroad roaring down,
In coop and in comb the fleece of his foam
Flutes and low to the lake falls home.

A windpuff-bonnet of fawn-froth
Turns and twindles over the broth
Of a pool so pitchblack, fell-frowning,
It rounds and rounds Despair to drowning.

Degged with dew, dappled with dew
Are the groins of the braes that the brook treads through,
Wiry heathpacks, flitches of fern,
And the beadbonny ash that sits over the burn.

What would the world be, once bereft
Of wet and of wildness? Let them be left,
O let them be left, wildness and wet;
Long live the weeds and the wilderness yet.

GERARD MANLEY HOPKINS

# OVERBOARD

What throws you out is what drags you in
What drags you in is what throws you
What throws you out is what drags
What drags is what throws you
What throws you drags
What drags throws
Throws drag
Thrags
Drags throw
What throws drags
What drags you throws
What throws is what drags you
What drags you in is what throws
What throws you out is what drags you
What drags you in is what throws you out
What throws you in is what drags you
What drags you out is what throws
What throws you out drags you
What drags throws you in
What throws drags you
Drags throw you
Thrags

MAY SWENSON

# WET

Wet wet wet
the world of melting winter,
icicles weeping themselves away
on the eaves
little brown rivers streaming
down the road
nibbling
at the edges of the tired snow,
    all puddled mud
    not a dry place to put
    a booted foot,
everything
    dripping
    gushing
    slushing
    slipping
and listen to that brook,
rushing
like a puppy loosed from its leash.

LILIAN MOORE

# FROM THE CATARACT OF LODORE

From its sources which well
   In the tarn on the fell;
   From its fountains
   In the mountains,
Its rills and its gills;
Through moss and through brake,
   It runs and it creeps
For a while till it sleeps
   In its own little lake.
And thence at departing,
Awakening and starting,
It runs through the reeds,
   And away it proceeds,
Through meadow and glade,
   In sun and in shade,
And through the wood-shelter,
   Among crags in its flurry,
   Helter-skelter,
   Hurry-skurry,
   Here it comes sparkling,
And there it lies darkling;
Now smoking and frothing
Its tumult and wrath in,
   Till, in this rapid race
     On which it is bent,
     It reaches the place
     Of its steep descent.

The cataract strong
Then plunges along,
Striking and raging
As if a war waging
Its caverns and rocks among;
Rising and leaping,
Sinking and creeping,
Swelling and sweeping,
Showering and springing,
Flying and flinging,
Writhing and wringing,
Eddying and whisking,
Spouting and frisking,
Turning and twisting
Around and around
With endless rebound:
Smiting and fighting,
A sight to delight in;
Confounding, astounding,
Dizzying and deafening the ear with its sound.

Collecting, projecting,
Receding and speeding,
And shocking and rocking,
And darting and parting,
And threading and spreading,
And whizzing and hissing,

And dripping and skipping,
And hitting and splitting,
And shining and twining,
And rattling and battling,
And shaking and quaking,
And pouring and roaring,
And waving and raving,
And tossing and crossing,
And flowing and going,
And running and stunning,
And foaming and roaming,
And dinning and spinning,
And dropping and hopping,
And working and jerking,
And guggling and struggling,
And heaving and cleaving,
And moaning and groaning;

And glittering and frittering,
And gathering and feathering,
And whitening and brightening,
And quivering and shivering,
And hurrying and skurrying,
And thundering and floundering;

Dividing and gliding and sliding,
And falling and brawling and sprawling,

And driving and riving and striving,
And sprinkling and twinkling and wrinkling,
And sounding and bounding and rounding,
And bubbling and troubling and doubling,
And grumbling and rumbling and tumbling,
And clattering and battering and shattering;

Retreating and beating and meeting and sheeting,
Delaying and straying and playing and spraying,
Advancing and prancing and glancing and dancing,
Recoiling, turmoiling and toiling and boiling,
And gleaming and streaming and steaming and beaming,
And rushing and flushing and brushing and gushing,
And flapping and rapping and clapping and slapping,
And curling and whirling and purling and twirling,
And thumping and plumping and bumping and jumping,
And dashing and flashing and splashing and clashing;
And so never ending, but always descending,
Sounds and motions forever and ever are blending,
All at once and all o'er, with a mighty uproar,—
And this way the water comes down at Lodore.

ROBERT SOUTHEY

# THE MAIN-DEEP

The long-rólling,
Steady-póuring,
Deep-trenchéd
Green billów:

The wide-topped,
Unbróken,
Green-glacid,
Slow-sliding,

Cold-flushing,
—On—on—on—
Chill-rushing,
Hush-hushing,

. . . . . Hush-hushing . . . . .

JAMES STEPHENS

# Oompah on the Tuba

## HEARING MUSIC

# RECITAL

Eskimos in Manitoba,
   Barracuda off Aruba,
Cock an ear when Roger Bobo
   Starts to solo on the tuba.

Men of every station—Pooh-Bah,
   Nabob, bozo, toff, and hobo—
Cry in unison, "In dubi-
   Tably, there is simply nobo—

Dy who oompahs on the tubo,
Solo, quite like Roger Bubo!"

JOHN UPDIKE

# A SUPERMARKET
# IN GUADALAJARA, MEXICO

In the supermercado the music
    sweet as the hot afternoon
wanders among the watermelons,
    the melons, the sumptuous tomatoes,
and lingers among the tequila bottles,
    rum bacardi, rompope. It
hovers like flies round the butchers
    handsome and gay as they dreamily
sharpen their knives; and the beautiful
    girl cashiers, relaxed
in the lap of the hot afternoon,
    breathe in time to the music
whether they know it or not—
    at the glossy supermercado,
the super supermercado.

DENISE LEVERTOV

# IN MEMORIAM JOHN COLTRANE

Listen to the coal
rolling, rolling through the cold
steady rain, wheel on

wheel, listen to the
turning of the wheels this night
black as coal dust, steel

on steel, listen to
these cars carry coal, listen
to the coal train roll.

MICHAEL STILLMAN

# PIANO

The perfect ice of the thin keys must break
And fingers crash through stillness into sound,
And through the mahogany darkness of the lake
Splinter the muteness where all notes are found.
O white face floating upwards amidst hair!
Sweet hands entangled in the golden snare,
   Escape, escape, escape,
  Or in the coils of joy be drowned.

What is the cabinet that holds such speech
And is obedient to caresses strange
As tides that stroke the long-deserted beach,
And gales that scourge the Peruvian mountain range?
O flesh of wood with flanks aglow with suns,
O quivering as at the burst of monstrous guns,
   Subside, subside, subside,
  Or into dust and atoms change.

Nor can the note-shaped heart, nor can the ear
Withstand your praise, O numbers more appalling
Than ringed and voyaging on the atmosphere
Those heavy flocks of fallen angels falling;
You strike with fists of heaven against the void
Where all but choiring music is destroyed,
   And light, and light, and light,
  Bursts into voice forever calling.

KARL SHAPIRO

# DUET

the day is so pretty

the umbrella is yellow

the day is so pretty
the sun is so shining

the umbrella is yellow
with white lace all around

the day is so yellow
the umbrella is so pretty
the sun is so all around
with white lace so shining

the umbrella is so yella
the sun is so pretty
with white all so shining
around lace so yellow umbrellow
with day is so yello sa yella
umbrella sa pretty sa yad

sa pretty sa yaddy
sa leylow sow lamu
brell white lace with shining
the sun is so all around

the day is so pretty
the umbrella is yellow
the day is so pretty
the sun is so shining
the umbrella is yellow
with white lace around

RUTH KRAUSS

# THE BELLS

## I.

Hear the sledges with the bells—
Silver bells!
What a world of merriment their melody foretells!
How they tinkle, tinkle, tinkle,
In the icy air of night!
While the stars that oversprinkle
All the heavens, seem to twinkle
With a crystalline delight;
Keeping time, time, time,
In a sort of Runic rhyme,
To the tintinnabulation that so musically wells
From the bells, bells, bells, bells,
Bells, bells, bells—
From the jingling and the tinkling of the bells.

## II.

Hear the mellow wedding bells—
Golden bells!
What a world of happiness their harmony foretells!
Through the balmy air of night
How they ring out their delight!—
From the molten-golden notes,

And all in tune,
What a liquid ditty floats
To the turtle-dove that listens, while she gloats
On the moon!
Oh, from out the sounding cells,
What a gush of euphony voluminously wells!
How it swells!
How it dwells
On the Future!—how it tells
Of the rapture that impels
To the swinging and the ringing
Of the bells, bells, bells—
Of the bells, bells, bells, bells,
Bells, bells, bells—
To the rhyming and the chiming of the bells!


III.

Hear the loud alarum bells—
Brazen bells!
What a tale of terror, now, their turbulency tells!
In the startled ear of night
How they scream out their affright!
Too much horrified to speak,
They can only shriek, shriek,
Out of tune,

In a clamorous appealing to the mercy of the fire,
In a mad expostulation with the deaf and frantic fire,
  Leaping higher, higher, higher,
  With a desperate desire,
  And a resolute endeavor
  Now—now to sit, or never,
 By the side of the pale-faced moon.
   Oh, the bells, bells, bells!
   What a tale their terror tells
    Of Despair!
   How they clang, and clash, and roar!
   What a horror they outpour
On the bosom of the palpitating air!
   Yet the ear, it fully knows,
    By the twanging
    And the clanging,
   How the danger ebbs and flows;
  Yet the ear distinctly tells,
    In the jangling
    And the wrangling,
   How the danger sinks and swells,
By the sinking or the swelling in the anger of the bells—
    Of the bells,—
  Of the bells, bells, bells, bells,
    Bells, bells, bells—
  In the clamor and the clangor of the bells!

IV.

Hear the tolling of the bells—
        Iron bells!
What a world of solemn thought their monody compels!
        In the silence of the night,
        How we shiver with affright
    At the melancholy menace of their tone!
        For every sound that floats
        From the rust within their throats
            Is a groan.
            And the people—ah, the people—
            They that dwell up in the steeple,
            All alone,
        And who tolling, tolling, tolling,
            In that muffled monotone,
        Feel a glory in so rolling
            On the human heart a stone—
    They are neither man nor woman—
    They are neither brute nor human—
            They are Ghouls:—
        And their king it is who tolls:—
        And he rolls, rolls, rolls,
            Rolls
        A paean from the bells!
    And his merry bosom swells
        With the paean of the bells!

And he dances, and he yells;
Keeping time, time, time,
In a sort of Runic rhyme,
  To the paean of the bells—
    Of the bells: —
Keeping time, time, time,
In a sort of Runic rhyme,
  To the throbbing of the bells—
    Of the bells, bells, bells—
  To the sobbing of the bells;
Keeping time, time, time,
  As he knells, knells, knells,
In a happy Runic rhyme,
  To the rolling of the bells—
    Of the bells, bells, bells: —
  To the tolling of the bells—
Of the bells, bells, bells, bells,
    Bells, bells, bells—
To the moaning and the groaning of the bells.


EDGAR ALLAN POE

# Grasshopper Copters Whir

## BIRDS, BEASTS,
## AND OTHER LIVING THINGS

# AIRPORT IN THE GRASS

Grasshopper copters whir,
Blue blurs
Traverse dry air,

Cicadas beam a whine
On which to zero in flights
Of turbojet termites,

A red ant carts
From the fusilage of the wren that crashed
Usable parts

And edging the landingstrip,
Heavier than air the river
The river
The rustbucket river
Revs up her motors forever.

X. J. KENNEDY

whippoorwill this

moonday into
(big with unthings)

tosses hello

whirling whose rhyme

(spilling his rings)
threeing alive

pasture and hills

E. E. CUMMINGS

# CATS

Cats walk neatly
Whatever they pick
To walk upon

Clipped lawn, cool
Stone, waxed floor
Or delicate dust

On feather snow
With what disdain
Lifting a paw

On horizontal glass
No less or
Ice nicely debatable

Wall-to-wall
Carpet, plush divan
Or picket fence

In deep jungle
Grass where we
Can't see them

Where we can't
Often follow follow
Cats walk neatly.

ROBERT FRANCIS

## *FROM* **THE SNAKE**

He drank enough
And lifted his head, dreamily, as one who has drunken,
And flickered his tongue like a forked night on the air, so
    black,
Seeming to lick his lips,
And looked around like a god, unseeing, into the air,
And slowly turned his head,
And slowly, very slowly, as if thrice adream,
Proceeded to draw his slow length curving round
And climb again the broken bank of my wall-face.

And as he put his head into that dreadful hole,
And as he slowly drew up, snake-easing his shoulders, and
    entered farther,
A sort of horror, a sort of protest against his withdrawing
    into that horrid black hole,
Deliberately going into the blackness, and slowly drawing
    himself after,
Overcame me now his back was turned.

I looked round, I put down my pitcher,
I picked up a clumsy log
And threw it at the water-trough with a clatter.

I think it did not hit him,
But suddenly that part of him that was left behind convulsed
   in undignified haste,
Writhed like lightning, and was gone
Into the black hole, the earth-lipped fissure in the wall-front
At which, in the intense still noon, I stared with fascination.

D. H. LAWRENCE

# THE CHESTNUTS ARE FALLING

First
the leaf
new and shiny,

then
the catkin's yellow
fur,

then the tiny
bud.

Now
the spiky swelling
burr,
splitting
spilling redbrown stain.

Thud!

LILIAN MOORE

# KINGFISHER

A flicker of blue
Under the sallows—
Over the shallows
A Kingfisher flew!

ELEANOR FARJEON

# BARRACUDA

Silver
War-lord
Of the warm reef
Long
Lithe
Lonely
Lurking
Beneath the quicksilver quiver
Of the sea's surface
A regal rapier
Lying inert
Ready to strike
Large jaws moving
Open and shut
Trying the water
With age-white teeth
And eyeing
The retreating man-fish
With centuries-old disdain

JOSEPH MACINNIS

off a pane)the
(dropp
ingspinson
his

back mad)fly(ly
who
all at)stops
(once

E. E. CUMMINGS

# THE CHIPMUNK

In and out the bushes, up the ivy,
Into the hole
By the old oak stump, the chipmunk flashes.
Up the pole

To the feeder full of seeds he dashes,
Stuffs his cheeks,
The chickadee and titmouse scold him.
Down he streaks.

Red as the leaves the wind blows off the maple,
Red as a fox,
Striped like a skunk, the chipmunk whistles
Past the love seat, past the mailbox,

Down the path,
Home to his warm hole stuffed with sweet
Things to eat.
Neat and slight and shining, his front feet

Curled at his breast, he sits there while the sun
Stripes the red west
With its last light: the chipmunk
Dives to his rest.

RANDALL JARRELL

l(a

le
af
fa

ll

s)
one
l

iness

E. E. CUMMINGS

# POEM

As the cat
climbed over
the top of

the jamcloset
first the right
forefoot

carefully
then the hind
stepped down

into the pit of
the empty
flowerpot

WILLIAM CARLOS WILLIAMS

# Hooray for the Show!

---

## ACTIVE ENTERTAINMENTS

# JENNY THE JUVENILE JUGGLER

Jenny had hoops she could sling in the air
And she brought them along to the Summerhill Fair.
And a man from a carnival sideshow was there,
Who declared that he needed a juggler.

And it's
   Oops! Jenny, whoops! Jenny,
   Swing along your hoops, Jenny,
   Spin a little pattern as you go;
Because it's
   Oops! Jenny's hoops! Jenny,
   Sling a loop-the-loop, Jenny,
   Whoops! Jenny, oops! Jenny, O!

Well, the man was astonished at how the hoops flew,
And he said, "It's amazing what some kids can do!"
And now at the carnival, Act Number Two
Is Jenny the Juvenile Juggler.

And it's
   Oops! Jenny, whoops! Jenny,
   Swing along your hoops, Jenny,
   Spin a little pattern as you go;
Because it's
   Oops! Jenny's hoops! Jenny,
   Sling a loop-the-loop, Jenny,
   Whoops! Jenny, oops! Jenny, O!

DENNIS LEE

# THE FOURTH

Oh
CRASH!

my
BASH!

it's
BANG!

the
ZANG!
Fourth
WHOOSH!

of

BAROOOM!

July
*WHEW!*

SHEL SILVERSTEIN

# SNEAKING IN THE STATE FAIR

As the fat sheriff who's taken
a week's vacation from his job as a clerk
and who shakes his billy like a threatening scepter
turns his horse and trots far the other way
boys swarm into the cyclone fence
like flies flat into a screen toward light
then scramble upward to the scarring top
where their wild fingers become careful and pluck
wires harsh with rusted barbs
as the sheriff rears and as hoofs throb closer
they grunt working up their dangling legs
clumsy, straining like bags of sand
as his club nears whacking the fence
demanding the meek admission fee
boys squatting at last on the swaying wires
bounce like frightened divers about to leap
from a distant board into a speck of a pool
then in a launching cheer they leap—
land hard scraping palms and knees,
the last sprawled like he'd never get up,
but with that red shout of "Stop those kids!"
they all pass a popcorn man on break
who goes along with the whacking and shouting
by yanking off his special cap and lurching
forward from his chair and his nap to
                              wink
as they slip into thin spaces in the crowd
that bumps slowly over sawdust toward the rides.

KEVIN FITZPATRICK

# TEN TOM-TOMS

Ten tom-toms,
Timpani, too,
Ten tall tubas
And an old kazoo.

Ten trombones—
Give them a hand!
The sitting-standing-marching-running
Big Brass Band.

UNKNOWN

# NARNIAN SUITE

*March for Strings, Kettledrums, and Sixty-three Dwarfs*

With plucking pizzicato and the prattle of the kettledrum
We're trotting into battle mid a clatter of accoutrement;
Our beards are big as periwigs and trickle with opopanax,
And trinketry and treasure twinkle out on every part of us—
     (Scrape! Tap! The fiddle and the kettledrum).

The chuckle-headed humans think we're only pretty poppetry
And all our battle-tackle nothing more than pretty bric-a-brac;
But a little shrub has prickles, and they'll soon be in a pickle if
A scud of dwarfish archery has crippled all their cavalry—
     (Whizz! Twang! The quarrel and the javelin).

And when the tussle thickens we can writhe and wriggle under it;
Then dagger-point'll tickle 'em, and grab and grip'll grapple 'em.
And trap and trick'll trouble 'em and tackle 'em and topple 'em
Till they're huddled, all be-diddled, in the middle of our caperings—
     (Dodge! Jump! The wriggle and the summersault).

When we've scattered 'em and peppered 'em with pebbles from
     our catapults
We'll turn again in triumph and by crannies and by crevices
Go back to where the capitol and cradle of our people is,
Our forges and our furnaces, the caverns of the earth—
     (Gold! Fire! The anvil and the smithying).

## 2.

### March for Drum, Trumpet, and Twenty-one Giants

With stumping stride and pomp and pride
We come to thump and floor ye;
We'll bump your lumpish heads today
And tramp your ramparts into clay,
And as we stamp and romp and play
Our trump'll blow before us—

(*crescendo*)    Oh tramp it, tramp it, tramp it, trumpet, trumpet
blow before us!

We'll grind and break and bind and take
And plunder ye and pound ye!
With trundled rocks and bludgeon blow,
You dunderheads, we'll dint ye so
You'll blunder and run blind, as though
By thunder stunned, around us—
By thunder, thunder, thunder, thunder stunned
around us!

Ho! tremble town and tumble down
And crumble shield and sabre!
Your kings will mumble and look pale,
Your horses stumble or turn tail,
Your skimble-skamble counsels fail,
So rumble drum belabored—

(*diminuendo*)    Oh rumble, rumble, rumble, rumble, rumble drum
belabored!

C. S. LEWIS

# MIME

on the black stage he
was in an imaginary box
mime mime mime mime mi

its inner surface stopped his
hand. the audience gasped
amazing amazing amazing ama

he climbed stairs that were
not there, walked and went
nowhere nowhere nowhere now

the real world was what his
head told his hands to delimit
in air in air in air in a

chill certain as glass. the
other world was fuzzy and
treacherous treacherous trea

he took a plane, it began
to fall, the passengers shrieked
help o God o help help he

the mime imagined a box.
his feet hit glass, the plane's
fall halted. up, up. praise be
mimesis mimesis mimesis mime

JOHN UPDIKE

# ORIGAMI FOR TWO

*Japanese art of paper folding*

Let's fold perhaps
a palace
of purple fruit paper
a paper place.

What plump apples!

And let's fold
in sheets of pink
peach fruit paper
balloons and then
a thin tissue fish.

No seedless grapes!

And perhaps we'll fold us
from red tissue
around the navels of oranges
a gondola.

The poor pale paper
from blue plums
we will simply fold
away.

Yes, a half dozen lemons!

And from the shredded
yellow tissue surrounding apricots
let's fashion streamers
for the voluptuous bed
of the melon.

PIETER DOMINICK

# FIREWORKS

First
A far thud,
Then the rocket
Climbs the air,
A dull red flare,
To hang, a moment,
Invisible, before
Its shut black shell cracks
And claps against the ears,
Breaks and billows into bloom,
Spilling down clear green sparks, gold spears,
Silent sliding silver waterfalls and stars.

VALERIE WORTH

# THE CIRCUS; OR ONE VIEW OF IT

Said the circus man, Oh what do you like
Best of all about my show—
The circular rings, three rings in a row,
With animals going around, around,
Tamed to go running round, around,
And around, round, around they go;
Or perhaps you like the merry-go-round,
Horses plunging sedately up,
Horses sedately plunging down,
Going around the merry-go-round;
Or perhaps you like the clown with a hoop,
Shouting, rolling the hoop around;
Or the elephants walking around in a ring
Each trunk looped to a tail's loop,
Loosely ambling around the ring;
How do you like this part of the show?
Everything's busy and on the go;
The peanut men cry out and sing,
The round fat clown rolls on the ground,
The trapeze ladies sway and swing,
The circus horses plunge around
The circular rings, three rings in a row;
Here they come, and here they go.
And here you sit, said the circus man,
Around in a circle to watch my show;
Which is show and which is you,

Now that we're here in this circus show,
Do I know? Do you know?
But hooray for the clowns and the merry-go-round,
The painted horses plunging round,
The live, proud horses stamping the ground,
And the clowns and the elephants swinging around,
Come to my show; hooray for the show,
Hooray for the circus all the way round!
Said the round exuberant circus man.
Hooray for the show! said the circus man.

THEODORE SPENCER

# At the
# Starting Line

## THE FEEL OF SPORTS

# SOMETIMES RUNNING

Sometimes running
to yes nothing and
too fast to look
where and at what
I stand and there
are trees sunning
themselves long a
brook going and
jays and jewelry
in all leafages
because I pause.

JOHN CIARDI

# CRYSTAL ROWE
## (Track Star)

Allthegirlsarebunched
togetheratthestarting
——— line ———

But

When the gun goes off

I

J

U
M
P

out ahead and
never look back
and
HIT
the

—T—— A —— P—— E——

a
WINNER!

MEL GLENN

# WATCHING GYMNASTS

Competing not so much with one another
As with perfection
    They follow follow as voices in a fugue
    A severe music.

Something difficult they are making clear
Like the crack teacher
    Demonstrating their paradigms until
    The dumb see.

How flower-light they toss themselves, how light
They toss and fall
    And flower-light, precise, and arabesque
    Let their praise be.

ROBERT FRANCIS

97

# LOVE

Too close
        to call,
too near
        the line
and in
        this game
between
        good friends
no one
        is sure
where out
        begins
or in
        side ends.

CAROL SUE MUTH

# CLOBBER THE LOBBER

                  slobs
          tennis       who
            with       have
           play        the
            to         urge
          need         to
           the         lengthen
         from          points
          us           with
       spare           lofty
          O            lobs!

FELICIA LAMPORT

99

# IN THE POCKET

Going backward
All of me and some
Of my friends are forming a shell   my arm is looking
Everywhere and some are breaking
In   breaking down
And out   breaking
Across, and one is going deep   deeper
Than my arm.   Where is Number One hooking
Into the violent green alive
With linebackers?   I cannot find him he cannot beat
His man   I fall back more
Into the pocket   it is raging and breaking
Number Two has disappeared into the chalk
Of the sideline   Number Three is cutting with half
A step of grace   my friends are crumbling
Around me the wrong color
Is looming   hands are coming
Up and over between
My arm and Number Three: throw it hit him in
the middle
Of his enemies   hit move scramble
Before death and the ground
Come up   LEAP STAND KILL DIE STRIKE


Now.

JAMES DICKEY

## _FROM_ ANGLO-SWISS,
## OR A DAY AMONG THE ALPS

Away she flies and he follows,
   Their out-thrust profiles glow,
Already their speed is fused with the frisson
   That expert skiers know;
Their hearts beat fast, beat faster,
   Where _she_ leads he will go
With a sibilant, swift and sugary hiss
   Over the perfect snow.

WILLIAM PLOMER

# THE SWIMMER'S CHANT

Stroke. Stroke.
Time that turn.
Stroke. Stroke.
Eyes burn.
Save strength
for last length.
Tired body
keep that beat.
Don't dare
think defeat.
Ace this race.
Win this meet.
Stroke. Stroke.
Arms are dead
but he's ahead.
Go, legs, go.
Fly, arms, fly.
Pull. Pull.
*Try*, don't die.
Let *him* cry.
Stroke. Stroke.
Burn that turn.
Lean. Clean.
Fast last lap.
Stroke. Stroke.
Swim to win.

Mean it. Breathe it.
GO FOR BROKE!
Stroke! Stroke!

The race is over. The race is done.
The team screams, "We've won! We've won!"
I'd like to shout and jump about
but I'm . . . . all . . . . . tuckered . . . out.

CAROL D. SPELIUS

# GREG HOFFMAN

| Lap | | | |
|---|---|---|---|
| | 1 | Swimming . . . . . . . . . . . | laps |
| | 2 | Is . . . . . . . . . . . . . . . . . . | such |
| | 3 | A . . . . . . . . . . . . . . . . . | pain, |
| | 4 | I . . . . . . . . . . . . . . . . . | wonder |
| | 5 | If . . . . . . . . . . . . . . . . | Coach |
| | 6 | Ramsey . . . . . . . . . . . . | would |
| | 7 | Mind . . . . . . . . . . . . . | if |
| | 8 | I . . . . . . . . . . . . . . . . . | just |
| | 9 | Stopped . . . . . . . . . . . . | in |
| | 10 | The . . . . . . . middle. | |

MEL GLENN

104

# THE SURFER

He thrust his joy against the weight of the sea;
climbed through, slid under those long banks of foam—
(hawthorn hedges in spring, thorns in the face stinging).
How his brown strength drove through the hollow and coil
of green-through weirs of water!
Muscle of arm thrust down long muscle of water;
and swimming so, went out of sight
where mortal, masterful, frail, the gulls went wheeling
in air as he in water, with delight.

Turn home, the sun goes down; swimmer, turn home.
Last leaf of gold vanishes from the sea-curve.
Take the big roller's shoulder, speed and swerve;
come to the long beach home like a gull diving.

For on the sand the grey-wolf sea lies snarling,
cold twilight wind splits the waves' hair and shows
the bones they worry in their wolf-teeth. O, wind blows
and sea crouches on sand, fawning and mouthing;
drops there and snatches again, drops and again snatches
its broken toys, its whitened pebbles and shells.

JUDITH WRIGHT

# POGOING

your intestines
spring up

                            but you swallow them
                            down

going up

like an auk
        a chicken
                a penguin

flapping   and keeping   the cracks
                   in mind

and never
        everlook
           at the sky

you might     lose your   b
                       a
                     l
                     a
                       n
                         c
                       e

CYNTHIA S. PEDERSON

# This Old Hammer

## POEMS TO WORK TO

# TIMES-SQUARE-SHOESHINE-COMPOSITION

I'm the best that ever done it
(pow pow)
    that's my title and I won it
    (pow pow)
I ain't lying, I'm the best
(pow pow)
    Come and put me to the test
    (pow pow)

I'll clean 'em till they squeak
(pow pow)
    In the middle of next week,
    (pow pow)
I'll shine 'em till they whine
(pow pow)
    Till they call me master mine
    (pow pow)

For a quarter and a dime
(pow pow)
    You can get the dee luxe shine
    (pow pow)
Say you wanta pay a quarter?
(pow pow)
    Then you give that to your daughter
    (pow pow)

I ain't playing dozens mister
(pow pow)
    You can give it to your sister
    (pow pow)
Any way you want to read it
(pow pow)
    Maybe it's your momma need it.
    (pow pow)

Say I'm like a greedy bigot,
(pow pow)
    I'm a cap'tilist, can you dig it?
    (pow pow)

MAYA ANGELOU

# BLACKSMITHS

Black-smocked smiths, smattered with smoke,
Drive me to death with din of their dints!
Such noise at night nor heard men never:
What knavish cry, and clattering of knocks!
The crooked cowards cry out "Col, col!"
And blow their bellows till all their brains burst.
"Huff, puff!" says that one, "Hoff, poff!" the other.
They're spitting and sprawling and spelling many spells,
They're gnawing and knocking and groaning together,
And holding hot things with their hard hammers.
Of a bull's hide are their big leather aprons,
Their calves are guarded against fiery sparks.
Heavy hammers they have that are handled hard,
Sharp strokes they strike on an anvil of steel.
"Bang, bang! Lash, dash!" go their answering crashes:
So doleful a dream let the devil dispel!
The boss takes a big piece of iron and binds it
To a tiny one, bangs it, and twangs out a treble.
"Tick, tock! Hick hock! Ticket, tockit! Tick tock!
Bang, bang! Lash dash!"—such a life they lead!
May Christ give all horse-shoers plenty of sorrow;
For these water-sizzlers, no man at night has his rest!

UNKNOWN

111

# THIS OLD HAMMER

This old hammer
Shine like silver,
Shine like gold, boys,
Shine like gold.

Well don't you hear that
Hammer ringin'?
Drivin' in steel, boys,
Drivin' in steel.

Can't find a hammer
On this old mountain
Rings like mine, boys,
Rings like mine.

I been workin'
On this old mountain
Seven long years, boys,
Seven long years.

I'm goin' back to
Swannanoa Town-o,
That's my home, boys,
That's my home.

Take this hammer,
Give it to the captain,
Tell him I'm gone, boys,
Tell him I'm gone.

TRADITIONAL

# *FROM* **THE SONG OF THE SHIRT**

Work—work—work
　Till the brain begins to swim;
Work—work—work
　Till the eyes are heavy and dim.
Seam, and gusset, and band,
　Band, and gusset, and seam—
Till over the buttons I fall asleep,
　And sew them on in a dream!

THOMAS HOOD

# CHEERILY MAN

*(Sea shanty for hoisting anchors)*

Haul all together!
   Chorus: *Cheerily man!*
Haul for good weather!
   *Cheerily man!*
She's light as a feather!
   *Cheerily man!*
Oh, hauley aye yeo!
   *Cheerily man!*

We'll haul again!
   *Cheerily man!*
With might an' main!
   *Cheerily man!*
Pay out more chain!
   *Cheerily man!*
Oh, hauley aye yeo!
   *Cheerily man!*

Chain stopper bring!
   *Cheerily man!*
Pass through the ring!
   *Cheerily man!*
Oh, haul and sing!
   *Cheerily man!*
Oh, hauley aye yeo!
   *Cheerily man!*

TRADITIONAL

# TINKER MAN

There never was yet a boy or a man
Who better could mend a kettle or pan,
A dipper, a skimmer, a pot, or a can
Than Jolly Old Roger, the Tinker Man.
Chee whing, chee whing, chee whing, chee whang,
Chee rattle, chee rattle, chee rattle, chee bang!

TRADITIONAL

# The Rusty Spigot Sputters

## TV AND TECHNOLOGY

# ONOMATOPOEIA

The rusty spigot
sputters,
utters
a splutter,
spatters a smattering of drops,
gashes wider;
slash,
splatters,
scatters,
spurts
finally stops sputtering
and plash!
gushes rushes splashes
clear water dashes.

EVE MERRIAM

# THE WATCH

I wakened on my hot, hard bed,
Upon the pillow lay my head;
Beneath the pillow I could hear
My little watch was ticking clear.
I thought the throbbing of it went
Like my continual discontent.
I thought it said in every tick:
I am so sick, so sick, so sick.
O death, come quick, come quick, come quick,
Come quick, come quick, come quick, come quick!

FRANCES CORNFORD

# PLAYER PIANO

My stick fingers click with a snicker
As, chuckling, they knuckle the keys;
Light-footed, my steel feelers flicker
And pluck from the keys melodies.

My paper can caper; abandon
Is broadcast by dint of my din,
And no man or band has a hand in
The tones I turn on from within.

At times I'm a jumble of rumbles,
At others I'm light like the moon,
But never my numb plunker fumbles,
Misstrums me, or tries a new tune.

JOHN UPDIKE

# THE DISASTER

We watch, fascinated,
as the horror is replayed
for us; over and over,
fast, then slower, then
fast again, over and over
and over, till we have
it by heart and it's no
longer a horror but a
shared, explicable event
we can talk about, shake
our heads at, walk away
from, as the patient,
soothing voice, cool and
competent and caring,
keeps repeating and
repeating . . .

BRUCE BENNETT

# WHEN HOWITZERS BEGAN

When howitzers began
   the fish darted downward
to weeds and rocks,
   dark forms motionless
in darkness, yet they were
   stunned and again
stunned
   and again and
again stunned, until their
   lives loosened, spreading
a darker darkness
   over the river.

HAYDEN CARRUTH

# TO SIT IN SOLEMN SILENCE

To sit in solemn silence in a dull, dark dock,
In a pestilential prison, with a life-long lock,
Awaiting the sensation of a short, sharp shock,
From a cheap and chippy chopper on a big black block!

W. S. GILBERT

# I Will Remember with my Breath

## THE MOTION OF THE MIND

# NIGHT PRACTICE

I
will
remember
with my breath
to make a mountain,
with my sucked-in breath
a valley, with my pushed-out
breath a mountain. I will make
a valley wider than the whisper, I
will make a higher mountain than the cry;
will with my will breathe a mountain, I will
with my will breathe a valley. I will push out
a mountain, suck in a valley, deeper than the shout
YOU MUST DIE, harder, heavier, sharper a mountain than
the truth YOU MUST DIE. I will remember. My breath will
make a mountain. My will will remember to will. I, suck-
ing, pushing, I will breathe a valley, I will breathe a mountain.

MAY SWENSON

# SONG

When your boyfriend writes you a letter
and you light up the air it's
love

When your boyfriend writes and you run
and the road runs with you and you run to the sea
the big blue beautiful bounding sea
and you tear it up the letter the beautiful letter
so your mother can't read it or find it no never
you jump with it into the sea
                              the sea
you jump with it into the mighty fine sea

When your boyfriend writes
When your boyfriend writes
and you light up the air
you light up the road
your shoes light up
your hair lights up it's
love oh-h-h-h-h-h-h it'-
s-s-s-s-s LOVE

RUTH KRAUSS

# A WHIRRING

A whirring, as of far-off music. Not the stir
of a wind, nor a leaf flir, nor plane whir, nor the rumble
of a train; but a whir as of wings of eagles
mingled with music of flutes; a parade about
to resonate into the spotlight of the street.

A whirring with flutes, and the thrumming of drumming,
and perhaps xylophones. From beyond the tombstones,
over the silent street came planing this whirring,
like an orchestra tuning up for a parade,
in accelerating rhythms of promise.

Would plumed valiant knights on rearing mounts,
bearing silken banners beckon me to come twirling
my wand of copper? Music whirring to *largo*
over the moving time sidewalk, immortalizing
the street, with peach-hued banners, and chars of flowers,

and argonaut vessels of gold: (the towers reeling).
Suddenly, it ceased; suddenly turned to a riddle.
Where had it veered in the middle of arrival?
(They knew I was waiting!) And why the retreat
into yesterday, and the grey street?

DAISY ALDAN

# THE STATUE

some greek statue
                pick
any one    leaning
                or curving
his back under
imaginary hasps


                turning
against the air
                bending
from hammer blows, blows
making him golden
making him white
                with boldness
                with
elegance
                asking


your eyes for approval
Taking it. You cannot
ignore what's there in your
bones, reaching
                within
you or turning
under the hasp
taking gold and whiteness
proudly from air, breathing
having the rest
fall away
the useless, the ugly

There in the blood
of your wrists of your thighs
the gold boy runs
without moving
moves without
                    touching

                    turns

as you move

          gazes

into your eyes.


                    ALEXANDRA GRILIKHES

# WINTER PAUSE: MT. LIBERTY, N.H.

No crunch of boots,
No wind now moves.
Your breathing slows.
Such stillness holds,
In trees, in sky,
You hear the ice
Return—and time
Speaks the sun's mind
With chill.
         While sound
Ticks snow
Around
You,
    an inner
Voice, like water
In blood, now beats
Each separate
Crystal that takes
The air and sparks
Your heart to move
With the old love—
Climbing again
To the sun's
Motion.

MARTIN ROBBINS

# THE STORY OF YOUR LIFE

always a new wrinkle
a new corner a new alley
a new twist

to be revealed
to be explored
to be gone into

a new secret
a new outrage

to be exhumed to be excused
to be explained to be exonerated

oh always and always
it is endless and it is endlessly
fascinating
who would have thought who would have dreamed
who would have imagined

oh it is endless
and you go on and you go on and you go on
        and you go on

and never
tire of it

BRUCE BENNETT

# ILLEGITIMATE THINGS

Water still flows—
The thrush still sings

though in
the skirts of the sky

at the bottom of
the distance

huddle
  . . . . echoing cannon!

Whose silence revives
valley after

valley to peace
as poems still conserve

the language
of old ecstasies.

WILLIAM CARLOS WILLIAMS

# INDEX OF TITLES

# INDEX OF FIRST LINES

# INDEX OF AUTHORS

Sitwell, Edith, 8
Southey, Robert, 47
Spelius, Carol D., 102
Spencer, Theodore, 90
Stephens, James, 51
Stevenson, Robert Louis, 38
Stillman, Michael, 57
Swenson, May, 23, 33, 45, 127

Thomas, Edward, 36

Updike, John, 30, 55, 87, 121

Williams, William Carlos, 78, 134
Wood, Sallie Burrow, 42
Worth, Valerie, 89
Wright, Judith, 105

# COPYRIGHT CREDITS

145

# LILLIAN MORRISON

is the author of six volumes of poetry and is well known for her collections of folk rhymes. Her fascination with poetry and movement led her to write *The Sidewalk Racer and Other Poems of Sports and Motion* and *The Breakdance Kids*, and to compile the poems for *Sprints and Distances*, an ALA Notable Book.

Ms. Morrison is a Phi Beta Kappa graduate of Douglass College, Rutgers University, and received a degree in library science from Columbia University. Formerly Coordinator of Young Adult Services for the New York Public Library, she is the recipient of the 1987 Grolier Foundation Award for her outstanding contribution to the stimulation of reading by young people. Ms. Morrison lives in New York City.